D1613428

# GEORG JENSEN

*This book is dedicated to all the silversmiths who, for the last 110 years,*
*have been upholding the legacy of Georg Jensen.*

# GEORG JENSEN

## REFLECTIONS

*Texts by*
MURRAY MOSS

*Photography by*
THOMAS LOOF

**RIZZOLI**
NEW YORK

New York · Paris · London · Milan

First published in the United States of America in 2014 by

*Rizzoli International Publications, Inc.*
300 Park Avenue South
New York, NY 10010
*www.rizzoliusa.com*
© 2014 Georg Jensen A/S
© 2014 Rizzoli International Publications

*Introduction and interior texts* © 2014 Murray Moss
*Preface* © 2014 David Chu
*Introduction* © 2014 Marc Newson

*Rizzoli Project Editors:* Dung Ngo and Philip Reeser
*Production:* Susan Lynch

*Editorial direction, additional text, and research:* Anne Taylor Davis
*Executive Producer of Photography:* Mariusz Skronski
*Research:* Stéphane Houy-Towner
*Research:* Ida Heiberg Bøttiger

ISBN: 978-0-8478-4321-3
Library of Congress Control Number: 2014941144

*Designed by NR2154:*
Jacob Wildschiødtz, Creative Director
Julie Lysbo Wildschiødtz, Art Director

Distributed to the U.S. trade by Random House, New York

Printed and bound in Italy

2014 2015 2016 2017 / 10 9 8 7 6 5 4 3 2 1

*All photography* © 2014 Thomas Loof except the following:
PAGE 8: Andrew Zuckerman
PAGES 12, 13, 18–19, 30, 40, 42–43, 48, 49, 61, 67, 68, 74, 76–77, 80, 100,
101, 105, 108–109, 122–123, 128, 134, 136, 145, 148, 156, 161, 168, 171, 176–177, 193,
226, 227 (ALL IMAGES BUT BOTTOM RIGHT), 228 (ALL IMAGES BUT BOTTOM LEFT), 230, 233,
AND 234 (ALL IMAGES BUT BOTTOM LEFT AND BOTTOM CENTER): Georg Jensen archive
PAGE 86: Karl Blossfeldt (1865–1932). *Aristolochia clematitis*, ca. 1928.
Image copyright © The Metropolitan Museum of Art. Image source: Art Resource, NY.
PAGE 189: Ken Haak/*Vogue* © Condé Nast Publications
PAGES 227 (BOTTOM RIGHT) AND 228 (BOTTOM LEFT): The Granger Collection, New York
PAGE 234 (BOTTOM LEFT): © 2005 Christie's Images Limited
PAGE 234 (BOTTOM CENTER): Image courtesy of the Philadelphia Museum of Art

# CONTENTS

# PREFACE

As Georg Jensen celebrates its 110th anniversary, I reflect on Georg's artistic bravery and entrepreneurial drive. Prior to opening a workshop in Copenhagen for the manufacture of jewelry in 1904, Jensen had completed an apprenticeship as a goldsmith, had graduated from the Royal Academy of Fine Arts with a degree in sculpture, and had had a ceramic piece titled *The Maid on the Jar* included in the Danish exhibition at the Exposition Universelle in Paris in 1900.

Shortly after the founding of the company, Georg created the *Blossom* teapot, designed the first flatware pattern, *Continental/Antik*, and by 1909 opened a Georg Jensen shop in Berlin, the first Jensen store outside Copenhagen.

He initiated the Jensen tradition of artistic collaborations, enlisting Johan Rohde, an established painter, and his brother-in-law Harald Nielsen as master designers in his silversmithy. Rohde is famous as the designer of the *Acorn* flatware pattern of 1916, which continues to be the most popular pattern in production today. Nielsen became the lead designer of the Art Deco period; many of his designs are also still in production.

I am struck by the genius of these men and how their designs exemplify a timeless point of view with a uniquely Nordic appreciation of silver as material and muse. I am grateful that others— art critics, design connoisseurs, curators, and collectors—share this appreciation of Georg Jensen. I am honored that museums of fine art and design all over the world have acquired Jensen for their collections. It is exciting to look at the creations of Jensen, Rohde, Nielsen, Sigvard Bernadotte, Henning Koppel, Vivianna Torun Bülow-Hübe, Verner Panton, and the company's many other designers and collaborators to see how each person imagined and reimagined Jensen in the context of their time and the sweep of design history.

In the words of Georg Jensen, "Do not follow fashion but be guided by the present if you want to stay young in the struggle." We embrace the past, explore the present, and look to the future. It is our intention to continue the founder's commitment to exciting and adventurous collaborations with new generations of artists, artists in every medium and from every country in the world.

*David Chu*

CEO, GEORG JENSEN

HENNING KOPPEL
Pitcher № 992
*1952*
*Silver with Pantone 1805C lacquer*

*Reimagined in 2013 by Jony Ive and*
*Marc Newson for the (RED) Auction,*
*this pitcher was customized with an*
*interior red lacquer.*

# FOREWORD

When thinking about the history of modern design, there are few enterprises in the twentieth century that truly stand out; Georg Jensen is one of the few that does. With such a rich heritage of iconic design, Georg Jensen is synonymous not only with craftsmanship but with multiple production, producing exquisite works that showcase techniques for which total mastery of material is paramount.

For me, handcraft has always been an important part of design, and it has played an important role in my own career. Having originally trained as a silversmith, I have an enormous respect for Georg Jensen, not only as a commercial entity but also as a company that champions both pure design and the importance of the individual craftsperson.

Pieces like the iconic *Pregnant Duck* serving pitcher, originally designed by Henning Koppel, are a case in point. Created in 1952, the work exemplifies modernism and, like most of the archival pieces, is still handmade to this day on the premises. Anachronistic yet still totally contemporary, the object is streamlined and flawless, belying the fact that it was made entirely by hand over many hundreds of hours, probably by the same person from beginning to end.

Sustainability has become more relevant than ever in the world of design, and the task for designers to meaningfully incorporate its ethics is more challenging than ever. My ultimate litmus test of sustainability is to aspire to create work that will not end up as landfill but rather become symbolic objects with inherent value that individuals bond with emotionally. Products made by Georg Jensen easily pass this test, creating value and history that will be cherished by generations to come.

*Marc Newson*

# FALLING IN LOVE

On occasion, people fall in love with objects. I certainly do.

And some of the people thus smitten become so with the immediacy of Shakespeare's Romeo.

When one first falls in love with Georg Jensen silver, I deduct it is generally love at first sight.

Even if the Romeo has a virgin eye—and little or no information or experience with the House of Jensen, the knowledge of its history, the designer, how it is made, how long it takes to make it, or how it might have come to represent supreme virtuosity in the art of silversmithing—there is something about the object of his affection (we might as well refer to it as his "Juliet") that captures his heart and makes him covet it in an instant.

Love at First Sight. "I'll take it."

In most cases, the history of Jensen unfolds much later, and over time our Romeo begins to understand why he fell in love with this particular Juliet.

And then (we can only imagine), should our Romeo live long with his Juliet, and his love for her not only continue but ever grow, there most likely will come a time when he can no longer remember why he fell in love—that moonlit evening having long ago waned.

Many couples take holidays in order to vacation from the familiar—the facts, so to speak—in order to spark the mind and body to summon the moment when, long ago, waiting in the dark, they saw a light break through yonder window and, seeing the object of their affection, cried out, but softly, "It is Juliet!"

This book departs from previous tours of Georg Jensen in that it is offered as a holiday to those in particular who have studied the facts surrounding Georg Jensen silver, and who once upon a time fell in love in an instant with Jensen, and may have loved Jensen for years, decades, or a lifetime, but who possibly have forgotten that first moment.

This book is my personal contemplation, an imagined truth, a rumination on the how and why, like a Romeo, one falls in love with Georg Jensen silver at first sight.

*Murray Moss*

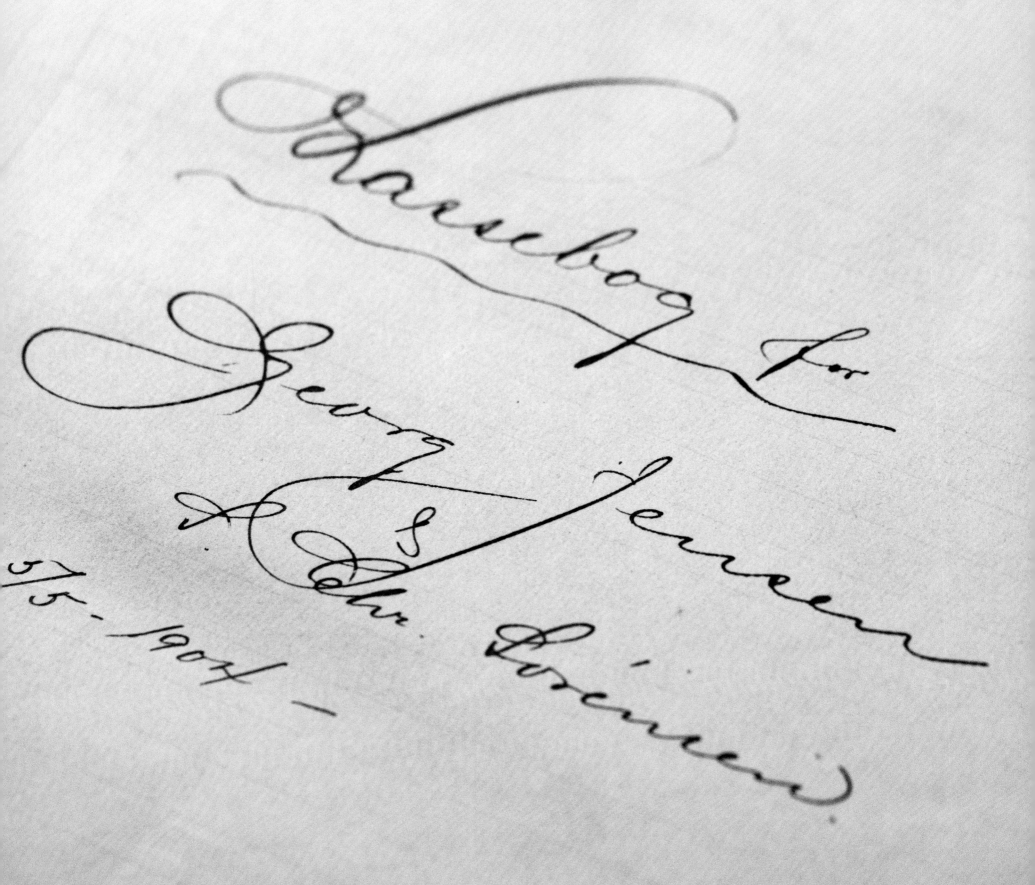

Kassebog for
Georg Jensen
& Chr. Sørensen
5/5 - 1904 -

Detail of Georg Jensen cash book
*1904*

*Opposite:*
Georg Jensen at the
Royal Academy of Art
*1892*

Plaster bust of Georg
Jensen by Willie Wulff
*1910*

# GEORG JENSEN

1866 - 1935

## THE SOUL OF JENSEN

FOUNDER / COLLABORATOR / SCULPTOR / ARTIST

*Jensen is recognized as the greatest silversmith of the past three hundred years. He referred to himself as "the silversmith sculptor," and his grave marker identifies him as Billedhugger or "Sculptor." Inspired by nature, Jensen compared the luster of his chosen material to the pure light of the Danish moon.*

To write a history of Georg Jensen silver is of course to write about the past.

The fact is several fine histories, of which one in particular could also serve as a very good catalogue raisonné, have already been written, relaying the facts of this 110-year-old company that, given its story, is in many ways the story of the twentieth century. Included are such cultural, political, and sociological upheavals as the emergence of the profoundly influential Arts and Crafts movement, the Industrial Revolution with its consequential mass production of goods and increase of services at affordable prices, the emergence of Charles Darwin's theory of survival of the species that prompted an interest in nature and human development, the globalization of ideas as a result of many international expositions that led to the blossoming of new artistic movements expressed differently throughout the Western world, and two devastating world wars.

Given that this ground is covered, I looked for what I believe has not been offered—a contemporary contemplation of a contemporary company. Granted, one with a spicy past, or as Jensen's Irish contemporary, playwright Oscar Wilde, had Lady Bracknell put it, "crowded with incident"—but tenaciously remaining relevant to us today. In the way that exceptional expressions in art of past eras continue to influence our present definition of beauty—such as early Greek and Roman depictions of the human form, seventeenth-century Dutch still-life painting holding a mirror up to life and to death, and in more recent times Abstract Expressionism and its eventual car crash with Warhol—the majority of artists' works executed by Jensen in silver over the past 110 years continues to resonate strongly with us today. These unique sculptures—for every work by Jensen, from brooch to spoon to fish server, is to me first and foremost sculpture—maintain their capacity to elicit from us a deep emotional response. In addition to

their being, in nearly all cases, an expression of nature— a nature curiously in sync with the digital age, appearing to have been almost algorithmically derived—Jensen sculpture has always intrigued me to a large extent because of it being silver, a singular material explored continuously through the decades by all Jensen artist/collaborators. This material is chosen not necessarily because of the perceived intrinsic monetary value but rather due to its unique alchemic properties that invite, or rather dare, one to forge it in a multiplicity of forms, each with the possibility to reveal something new.

Those fortunate enough to acquire exceptional pieces of Georg Jensen hollowware for their homes today, or to adorn themselves with Georg Jensen jewelry, or to own a Jensen timepiece, I believe do so for the same reason one might travel with Louis Vuitton luggage or wear Chanel—these objects embody values, both aesthetic as well as what we deem quality, which we hold dear today, even though the designs might have been introduced over a century ago.

Like the Danish monarchy, established over one thousand years ago but defined today by a progressive royal family, Georg Jensen proudly embraces its legacy, while communicating it in today's vernacular.

In every calibrated blow of the hammer to the silver, every weld executed as if by a surgeon, every sensual curve measured and mastered by the hand, eye, and heart of a Jensen sculptor/silversmith today, lives the lineage of Georg Jensen. The deafening noise of hand-hammering silver wakes up the past.

This cannot be explained through historical facts alone; for example, how can one give a date, a time, or a place to passion?

Georg Jensen hallmark
*1904–1908*

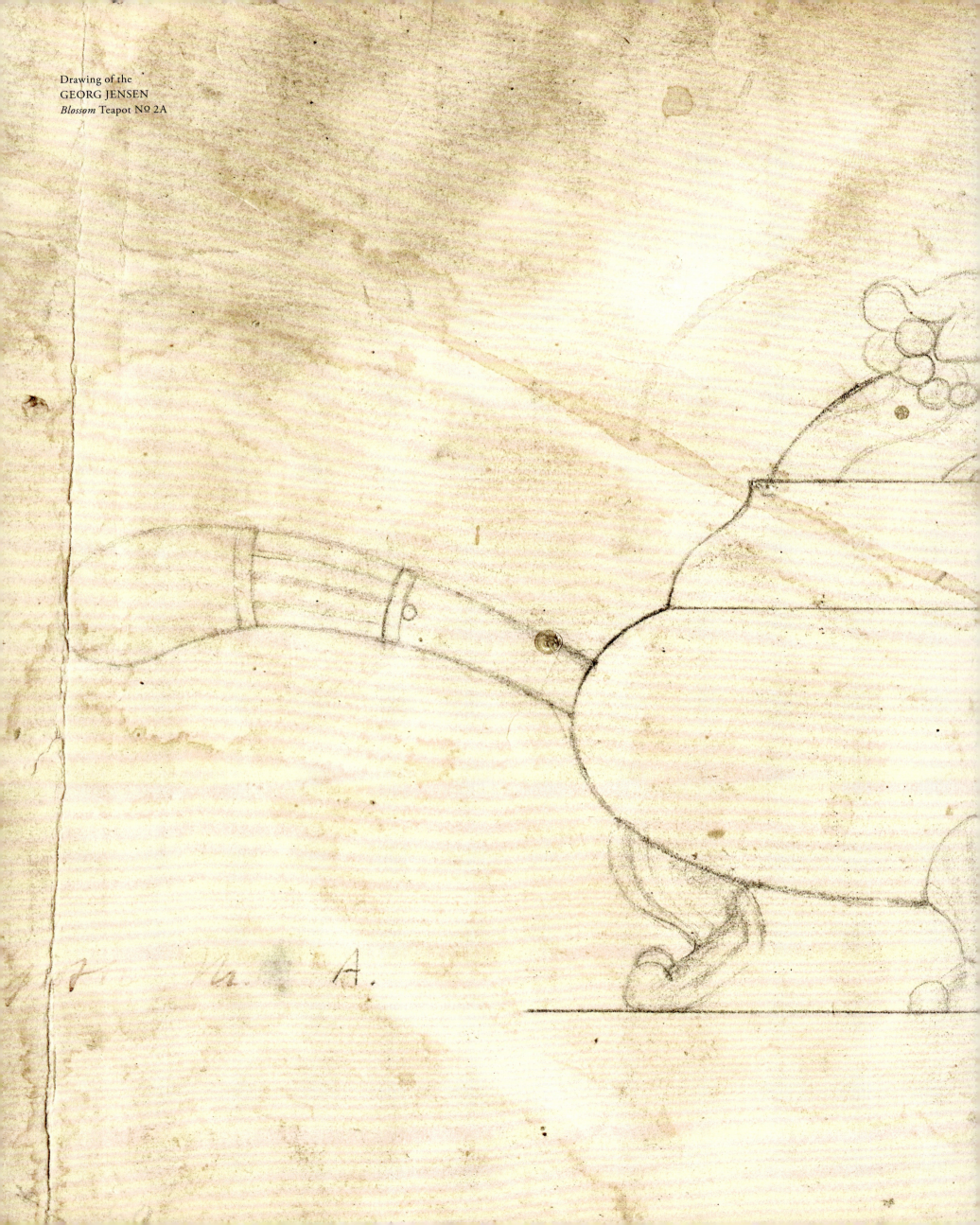

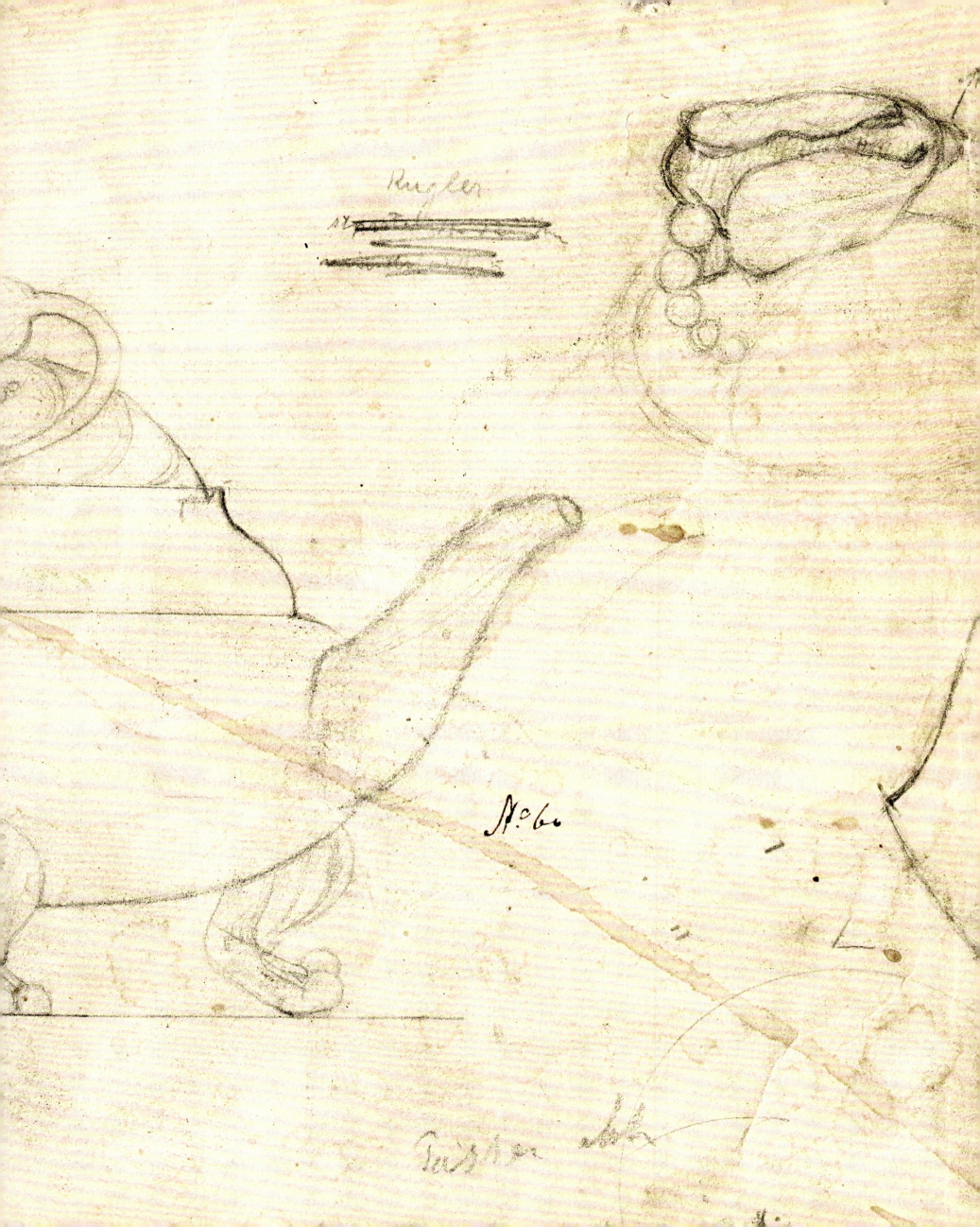

GEORG JENSEN
*Blossom* Teapot № 2A
*1905*
*Silver and ivory*

GEORG JENSEN
Bonbonnière
*1908*
*18-karat gold, sapphire, and moonstones*

GEORG JENSEN
Tea Caddy № 137 (lid detail)
*1912*
*Silver and amber*

GEORG JENSEN
*Grape* Bowl № 264A
*1918*
*Silver*

# 1918 *GRAPE* BOWL

Designed by the master himself in 1918, the sterling-silver bowl with grape ornamentation is perhaps the best-kept secret of Radical Design. The neo-Baroque stem demonstrates and celebrates the near-Divine potential of man—emerging exuberantly, master-crafted from a simple disc of silver in as tornado-like a spin as Bernini's swirling columns of 1625 for Saint Peter's Basilica in the Vatican. Then, suddenly, in a heartbeat, without warning, Georg Jensen puts the brakes on spectacle, and the richly adorned column miraculously blossoms into a reductive, seductive, fine Minimalist bowl— a time machine giving us an uncanny look into the future, when the movement would be defined as Danish Modern.

*Opposite:*
GEORG JENSEN
Tea Caddy Nº 46
*1914*
*Silver and amber*

# THEDAASE · Nº 46 ·

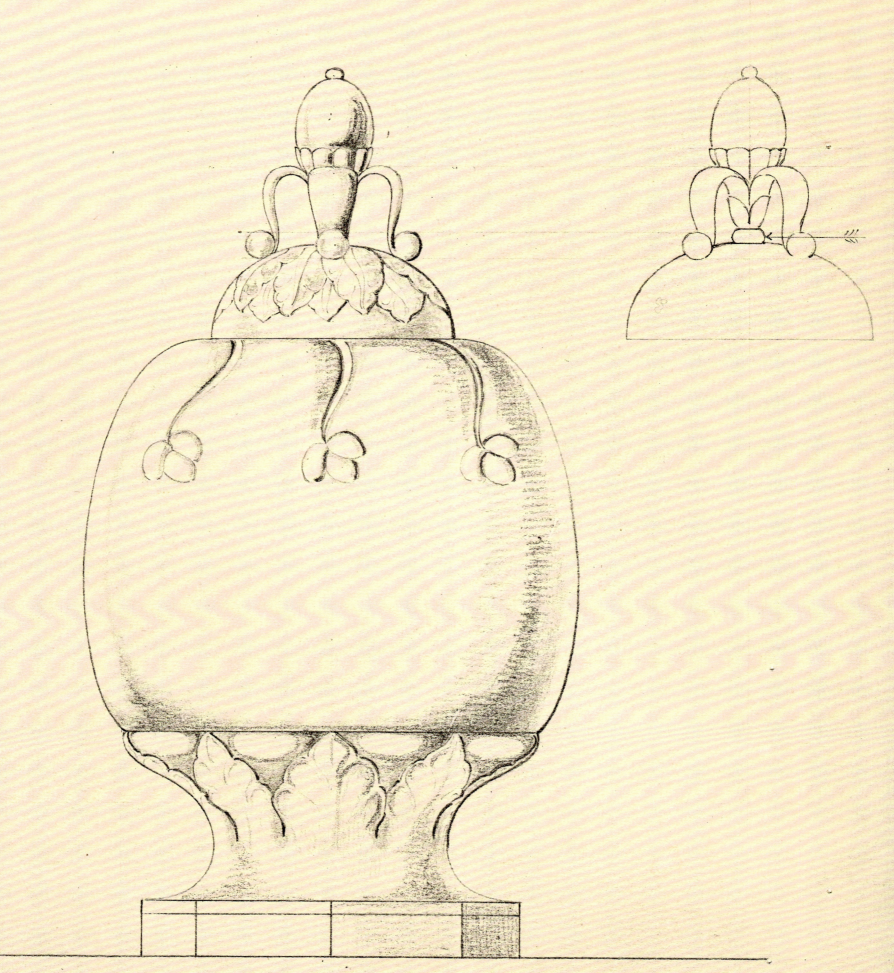

GEORG JENSEN
Chocolate Pot № 460B/
Paris № 15
*1926*
*Silver and rosewood*

*Opposite:*
GEORG JENSEN
Chocolate Pot № 460B/
Paris № 15 (lid detail)
*1926*
*Silver and rosewood*

GEORG JENSEN
*Blossom* Soup Ladle № 84/151
*1919*
*Silver*

Drawing of the
GEORG JENSEN
*Blossom* Coffee Pot № 2D

Drawing of the
GEORG JENSEN
Jardinière № 1397

FRUGT

BLOMSTER BLOMSTER BLOMSTER

FRUGT

*N.*

GEORG JENSEN
Jardinière Nº 1397
*1926*
*Silver*

# JOHAN ROHDE

1856 — 1935

## THE NATURALIST

PAINTER / FURNITURE DESIGNER / MAESTRO OF SILVER
FLATWARE AND HOLLOWWARE

*Showing Rohde's mastery at simplification and modernization of design, the Acorn flatware pattern of 1915 remains one of Georg Jensen's most famous and beloved styles almost one hundred years after its first production.*

Like Blossfeldt and the New Objectivity that emerged post-1914, artist Johan Rohde's designs for Georg Jensen were a departure from the extravagant, florid, untempered nature motif of the Art Nouveau period. Creating a bridge between this era, which by 1914 had exhaustively celebrated ornamentation, and what would emerge shortly thereafter in the mid-1920s, as the Modern movement, with its defining characteristic being simplicity, Rohde's drawings for Jensen were in fact similar to an earlier bridge in art, Mannerism, which, evolving four hundred years prior, at the end of the High Renaissance, was the transition necessary to reach the Baroque.

Arguably, Rohde created an interlude in design that might be termed Mannerist Modernism.

Sixteenth-century Mannerism sought to represent an ideal of beauty rather than depict literal images of nature to accomplish that goal, employing distortion and exaggeration of proportions. Giving expression to the artist's idea rather than to true nature, by means of asymmetrical compositions and elongated forms, Mannerism, while technically masterful, embraced disquieting compositions that were emotional in spite of their simplicity, and that, in form, were in certain instances close to those silhouettes of a future Modigliani.

Looking at Rohde's amazing Jug No. 432, designed in 1920 but not put into production until 1925, one sees a radical departure from all that came before; its sensual shape, almost figural, gives a palpable sense of tense, controlled emotion and is emblematic of an ideal of female beauty characterized by elongated proportions; in form, if abstracted, it is close to Joachim Wtewael's 1616 Mannerist painting of Andromeda, in his masterwork *Perseus and Andromeda*.

As had occurred in art four hundred years earlier, Rohde's Mannerist Modernism, a prescient glimpse of the future, emphasized complexity, albeit subtly embedded in an outward simplicity, and great virtuosity over naturalistic representation.

Although vestiges of nature remained—especially in the judicious placement here and there of his beloved acorn motif, such as the small ornament on the jug pictured, placed discreetly at the point where the handle joins the body—decoration, as Rohde anticipated before others, was gone.

After all, Adolf Loos had in fact already made ornament nothing less than a crime.

Rohde began his relationship with Jensen as a client in 1906, commissioning a coffee service of his own design to be executed by the newly established manufactory. The relationship grew and in 1913 Rohde began supplying designs to the Georg Jensen workshop under a contractual agreement that would permit them to be offered under the Georg Jensen mark. Of all of the Rohde designs that were produced, his greatest success was, and continues to be, the cutlery pattern *Acorn*, introduced in 1915. It's uncanny, that pattern's likeness to an ancient Greek architectural order, as expressed in the Doric, Ionic, and Corinthian degrees of ornament. Rohde revives an aesthetic archetype that introduces a historic order, balance, and coded decoration—in other words, temperance—to everyday functional objects, transforming them into a very refined art. The *Acorn* pattern ornament at the tip of each piece of cutlery from that collection clearly, upon inspection, to me is a direct reference to the scrolls on Ionic capitals, as the fluted stems of the cutlery suggest the supportive columns of that order.

Design, like all art forms, has a family tree, a lineage from which it branches out, responding to the times. Johan Rohde knew the history of art—and in understanding it to be his history as well brought design forward through his objects for Georg Jensen, which reflect our classical past while carrying us to a new dimension. Like any adventurer or pioneer, Rohde's vision expanded the Known World.

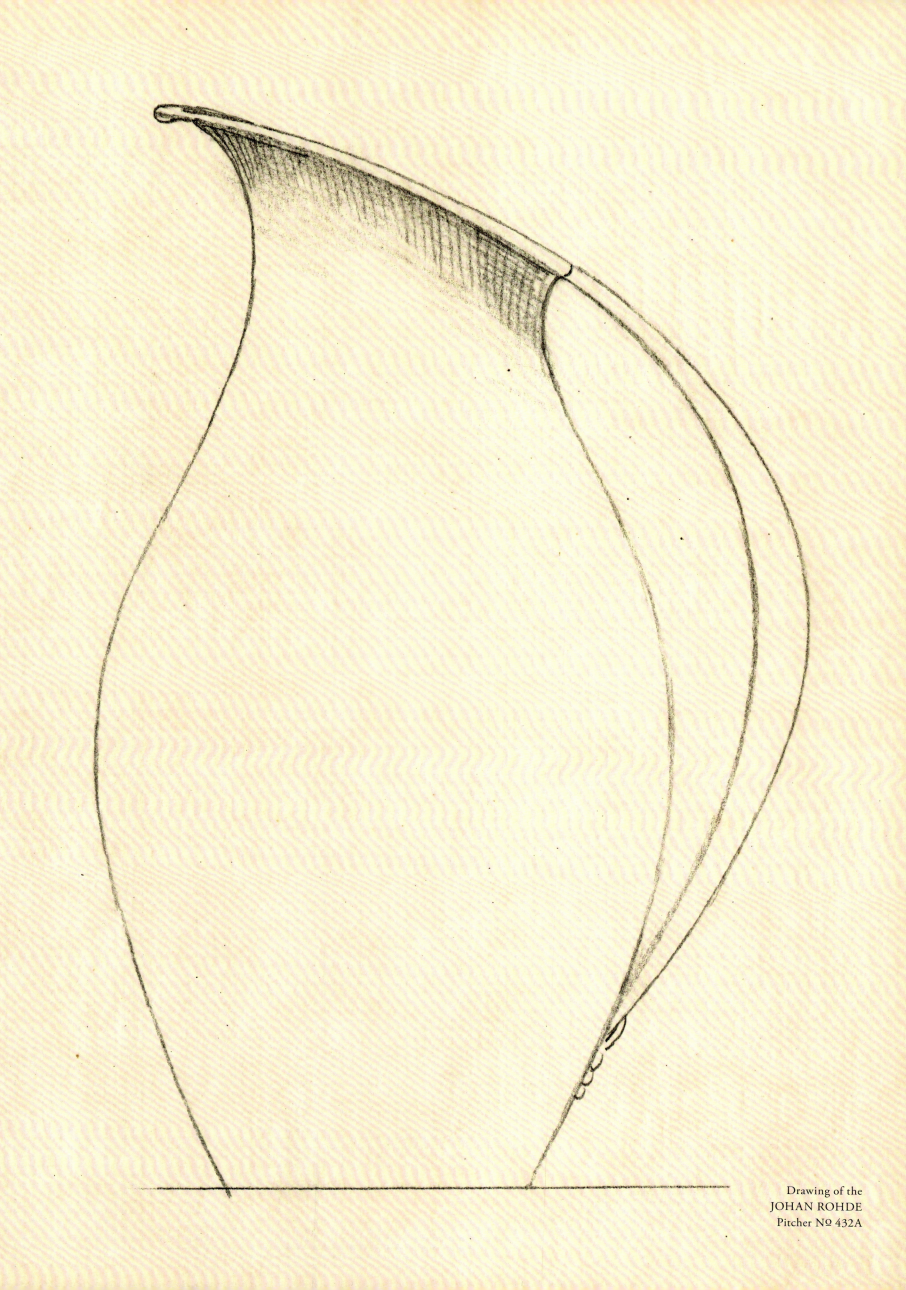

Drawing of the
JOHAN ROHDE
Pitcher № 432A

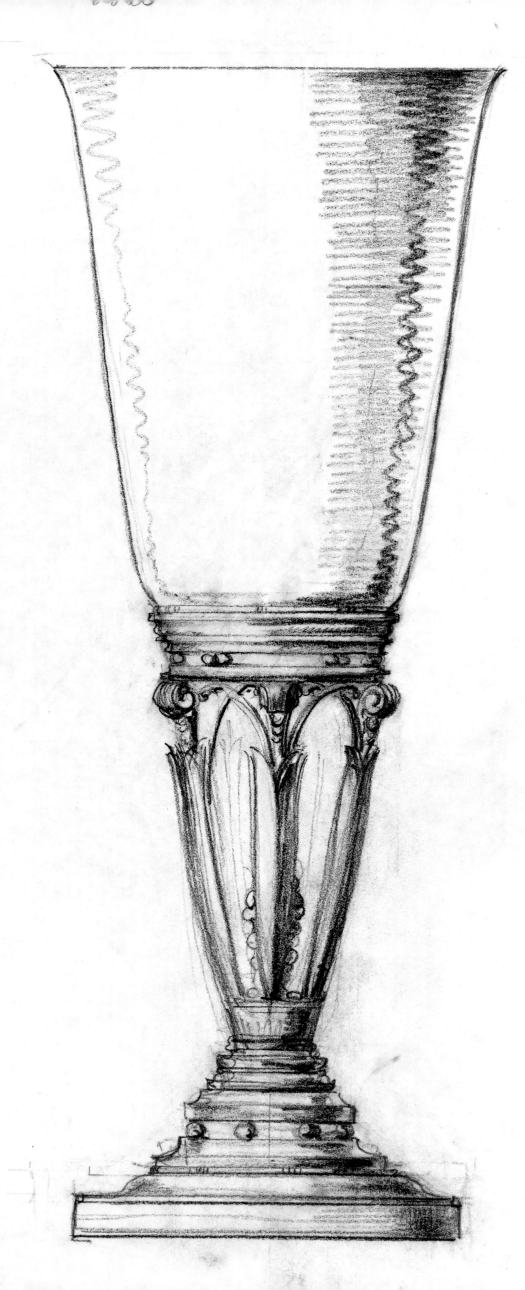

Drawing of the
JOHAN ROHDE
Vase № 250

JOHAN ROHDE
Vase № 250
*1928*
*Silver*

# VIRTUOSITY

Like the classical orders that governed ancient Greek architecture, Georg Jensen silver—especially the early works in jewelry modeled by Mr. Jensen himself— appears to me to follow a highly structured system of pleasing proportions that relate individual decorative elements to the entire work at hand, be it a brooch, a bracelet, or a buckle. Like the Doric, Ionic, and Corinthian orders— each established by certain modules similar to the intervals in music, creating a grammar for an audience attuned to its language and therefore bringing certain expectations—each component of a Jensen piece appears to be sized and arranged according to an overall proportioning system. The result is a representation of natural forms tempered in each case by degree of complexity of ornamentation, but always executed with rigor and a precision requiring virtuosity, whether simpler and therefore more Doric than Corinthian, or embellished and therefore more Ionic than Doric.

Is it possible that a proportional system of ancient Greek origin is the root of Danish Modernism?

JOHAN ROHDE
*Acorn* Flatware Nº 62
*(Asparagus Tongs, Strawberry Spoon,
Large Soup Ladle, Mixing Spoon,
Cucumber Spoon, Tomato Knife,
Cucumber Fork, Saltcellar, Salt Spoon,
Grape Shears, Grapefruit Knife, Orange Knife,
Herring Fork, Oyster Fork, Cheese Scoop, Tea Egg,
Canapé Server, Large Perforated Pastry Server,
and Melon Set)*
*1915*
*Silver, ebony, dark horn, and blue enamel*

Drawing of the
JOHAN ROHDE
*Acorn* Cutlery Nº 62 (detail)

*Opposite:*
JOHAN ROHDE
*Acorn* Cutlery Nº 62 (detail)
*1915*
*Silver*

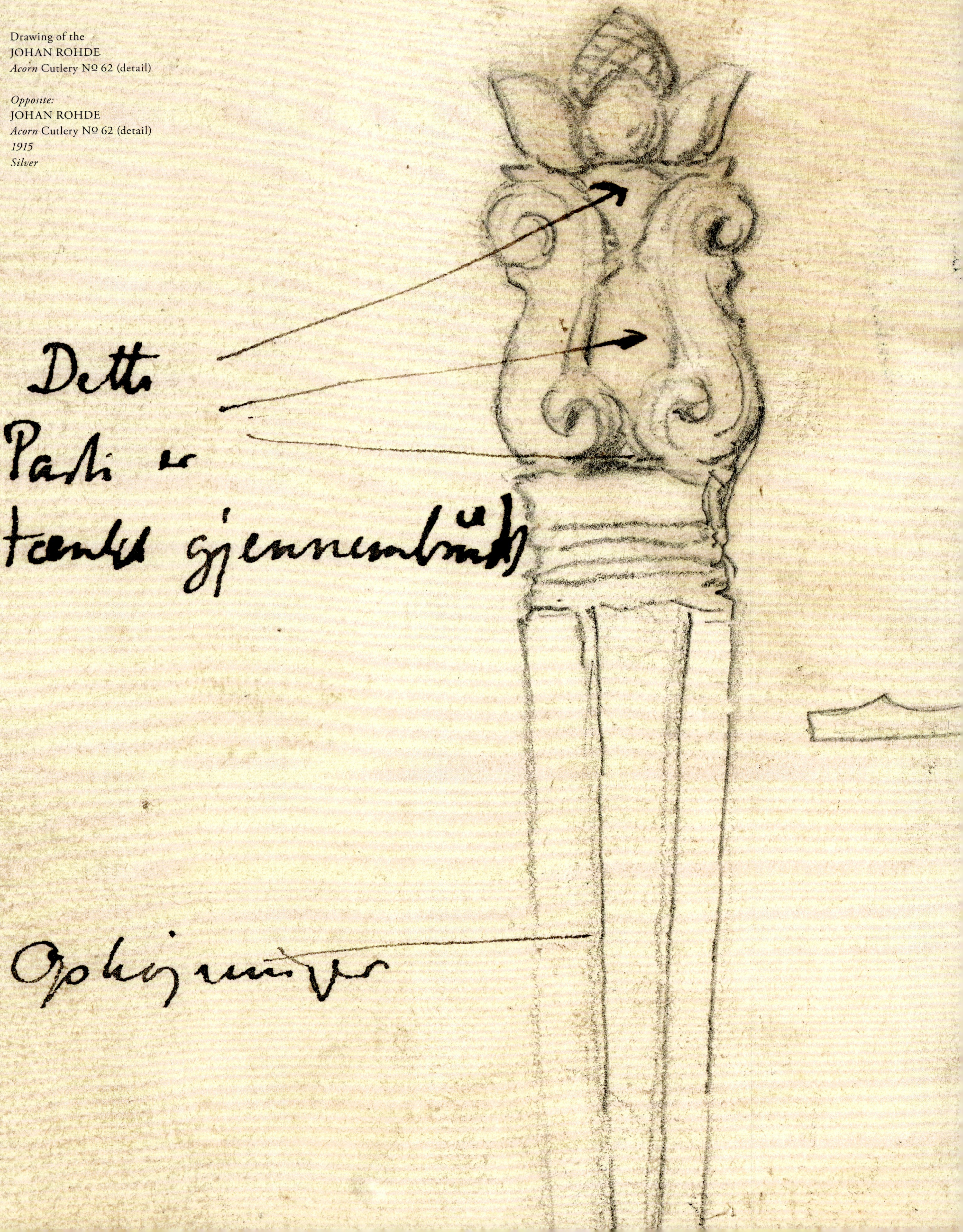

Blik

Indvendige Lavie

Længden af lave
Kugler

Kugle

Design drawings from
the Georg Jensen archive

JOHAN ROHDE
Candelabrum № 481B
*1926*
*Silver*

Drawing of the
JOHAN ROHDE
Table Clock № 333

JOHAN ROHDE
Table Clock № 333
*1919*
*Silver on black onyx base*

JOHAN ROHDE
Table Lamp № 208
*1917*
*Silver*

*Opposite:*
GEORG JENSEN
Bell Push № 109
*1919*
*Silver*

OLIV...RCEY
Graveur Imprimeur Conseil
96, rue du Bac, 75007 Paris

JOHAN ROHDE
*The King's Bowl* № 250A
*1917*
*Silver*

*Opposite:*
JOHAN ROHDE
Table Clock № 333 (detail)
*1919*
*Silver*

# BLOSSFELDT

Karl Blossfeldt, whose life spanned nearly the exact years as Georg Jensen's, was also a sculptor, as well as a university professor who taught modeling based on a study of living plants. Having spent nearly his entire adult life photographing plants and plant segments, Blossfeldt hoped to ignite a rejuvenation of imaginativeness from a new naturalism. His now-famous photographs, published for the first time in the 1928 book *Urformen der Kunst* (Art Forms in Nature), are best described by Gert Mattenklott in his book *Karl Blossfeldt—Photographs*: "Nature is viewed as art, and art is viewed as nature. The sentimental to-and-fro between nature and art vacillates between stressing the artistic in nature and the vegetal in art."

Like Blossfeldt, in the period immediately following the First World War, Georg Jensen recognized in the natural world artistic forms that arose from biological necessity, or evolution. Arguably, this was a result of the New Objectivity, the term used at that time to characterize the emergence of a new, stark realism that manifested itself in a more sober portrait of contemporary society. In the various arts, this included removing objects from their context, and aiming toward a sharply defined imagery, more static by far than the prewar Art Nouveau frenzy. The precision, the sobriety, the fine reserve that is so evident in Jensen silver at that time, I believe, suited Jensen's view of Nature as something beautiful and indeed magical, but to be controlled. This is why, perhaps, Jensen invented his own Nature so that, like Geppetto, he could pull the strings.

What Mattenklott wrote of Blossfeldt, he might just as easily have written of Jensen—that "Nature is viewed as art"—and in the case of silversmithing that meant Nature yielding to the artist's loud and fierce planishing hammer.

How fortuitous that the hammer was swung by Georg Jensen.

Silver Flowers for Georg Jensen's
*Blossom* Cutlery № 84

# NARCISSUS

Of the hundreds, perhaps thousands, of Nature-inspired pseudo-flora Jensen and his coterie of early twentieth-century artists-as-silversmiths rendered in polished silver, absent is the Narcissus.

Narcissus, the handsome young man in Greek mythology who was cursed to fall in love with his own reflection.

We can imagine a handsome young Georg, raised in a land lulled to sleep each night on the fables of Hans Christian Andersen, becoming masterful in his craft, but perhaps reticent, constantly looking into the silver where, somewhere beneath the surface, he was forever returning his own gaze.

Perhaps that is part of the obsessive stylistic repetition of that early body of Jensen work, each model different but, being Nordic, in the way snowflakes differ from one another.

Those many beautiful brooches and buckles and bracelets and earrings, with their flowers and shafts of hay seemingly wafting to the melodies of the Nutcracker Suite, some poignantly contorted due to their determination to remain safely and obediently tucked within their maker's frame, all embody a calm grace, a chastity. There is in each piece a painful restraint, a hesitation, an innocent's modesty, a blush, a humility, a gentle warning or, shall we say, a fine reserve, uncommon in adornment today.

I think we are being reminded by the boy, Georg, reflected in the man, Mr. Jensen, in ever so hushed a bedtime voice, of the cautionary tale of Narcissus.

HARALD NIELSEN
*Powder Box* № 153
*1920*
*Silver*

GEORG JENSEN
Pendant № 1
*1904*
*Silver and black agate*

1

1

1

Nr. 1

Drawing of the
GEORG JENSEN
Pendant № 1

HARALD NIELSEN
Champagne Goblet № 532E
*1928*
*Silver*

---

# HARALD NIELSEN

1892 – 1977

## THE MANNERIST

PAINTER / ILLUSTRATOR / DIRECTOR OF THE SMITHY
AND ARTISTIC DIRECTOR

*Nielsen created Art Deco masterpieces,
in addition to rendering the precise
drawings used by the silversmiths for pieces
by Jensen and Rohde.*

A period referred to as "Between the Wars," any wars, by definition suggests only a temporary lull in conflict, during which time a series of events are gathering momentum that eventually lead to a resumption of hostilities.

A dysfunctional transition is implied, in this case, in the word "between"—a patchwork truce rather than a lasting treaty—and with it an unease and/or uncertainty touching all aspects of life. During such a period, Art, always an advance scout, generally makes a shift from what had been the status quo to the new reality (whatever that may be), and is often the first venue to articulate where the world is going next, and what it might look like.

Harald Nielsen thrived artistically between the wars—in his case, the years between 1918 and 1939. Perhaps he was a person who, against the common grain, embraced change, inspired by the real opportunities that are momentarily made possible when hollow traditions, defunct archetypes, fall from grace and leave a series of political, social, and aesthetic voids that enterprising individuals, if sufficiently talented and sufficiently empowered to act quickly, may fill.

Harald Nielsen, in the years "in between"—being more than sufficiently talented, and empowered with the Jensen organization and credibility and extraordinary technical and industrial capabilities at his service, along with a loyal audience—filled the void left by a no-longer "belle" époque with a new visual design language more suitable for a "functionaliste" époque, which he was able not only to intuit but also to draw.

Harald Nielsen, in the years "in between," designed Modernism.

Like his brother-in-law Georg Jensen and like Henning Koppel and Johan Rohde, Harald Nielsen set out to be a fine artist, a painter. Beginning work as an apprentice at the Jensen workshops in 1909, Nielsen rose within the company to become artistic director and in 1954 was made a director of the corporation.

Although his early work abided by the tenets of Art Nouveau, he has been quoted as saying later, "Bunches of grapes weren't really me."

Inspired by a confluence of circumstances—Georg Jensen's willingness to exploit the potential of machinery, having no qualms about employing a hybrid manufacturing process that included both handcraft and industrial craft; and the public's fascination at the time with Ancient Egypt, after the discovery of Tutankhamen's tomb in 1922—Nielsen created his *Pyramid* cutlery pattern in 1926. Although certainly in the zeitgeist, *Pyramid* broke with all earlier traditions to become the first design written in the new Modern language, being more noteworthy for ushering in a new industrial art than as a bestseller in the Egyptian Revival style. In his book *Georg Jensen: Silver & Design*, Thomas C. Thulstrup writes, "Pyramid fulfilled the need for a cutlery service which corresponded with the aesthetics of the period and yet preserved the weight and fullness associated with silverware. It was an added bonus that the pattern was suitable for execution in a modern manufacturing setup." He concludes, "Pyramid was thus well suited for large and profitable production."

Harald Nielsen had a long and prolific career at Georg Jensen, creating a new definition of Industrial Designer as not only form-giver and problem-solver but also engineer and artist combined, with no border.

It is said that each age creates its own Leonardo.

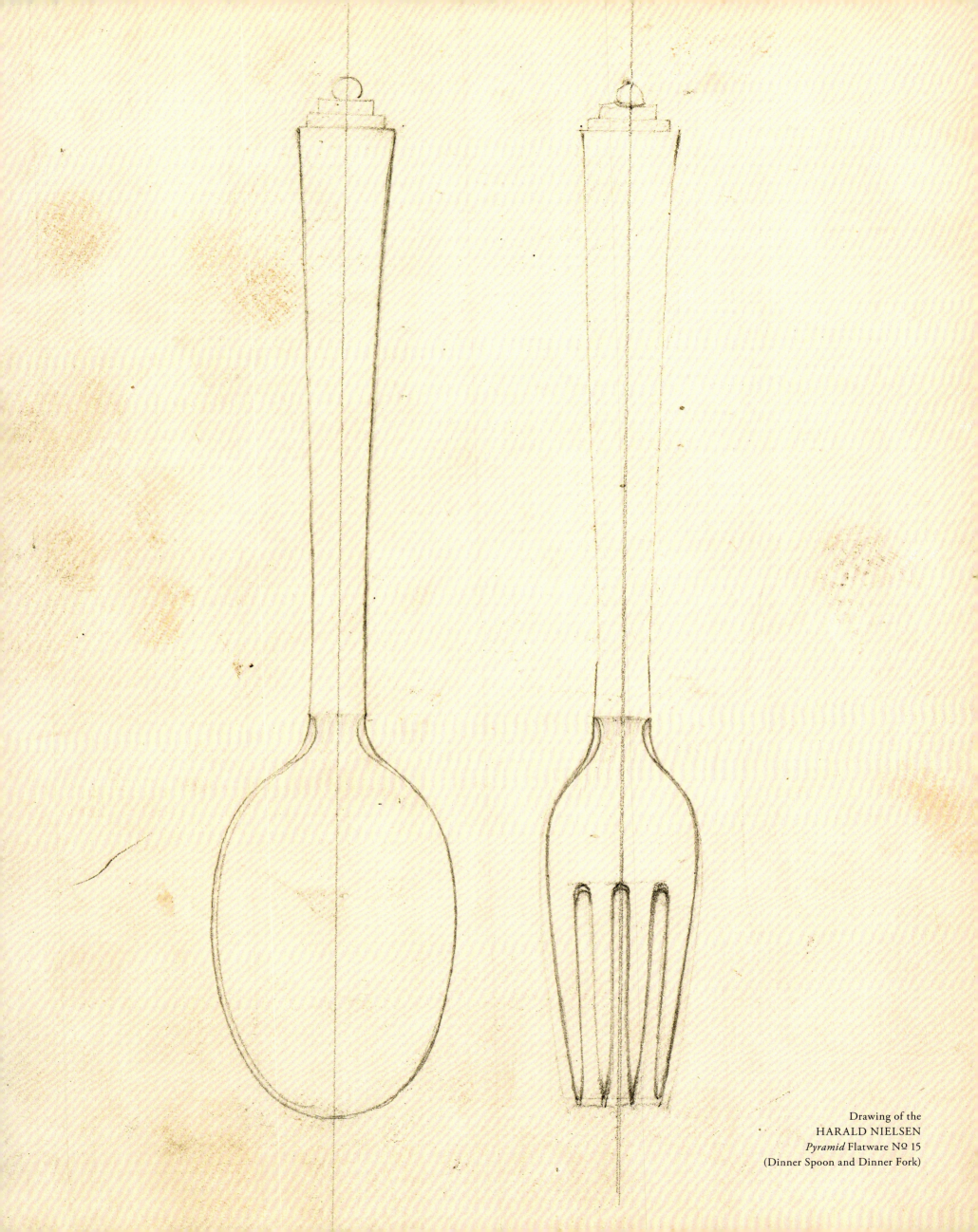

Drawing of the
HARALD NIELSEN
*Pyramid* Flatware № 15
(Dinner Spoon and Dinner Fork)

HARALD NIELSEN
Candelabrum № 630A
*1930*
*Silver*

Tea Service № 600B
(Teapot, Sugar Bowl
with Lid, and Creamer)
*1930*
*Silver and ebony*

Drawing of the
HARALD NIELSEN
Teapot № 600

HARALD NIELSEN
*Pyramid* Flatware № 15
(Dinner Knife, Dinner Fork,
and Dinner Spoon)
*1930*
*Silver*

*Pyramid* Hollowware № 632
(Saltcellar and Mustard Pot)
*1930*
*Silver with blue enamel*

*Opposite:*
HARALD NIELSEN
Candelabrum № 751
*1935*
*Silver*

HARALD NIELSEN
*Candelabrum* № 865 (detail)
*1938*
*Silver*

*Opposite:*
HARALD NIELSEN
*Candelabrum* № 865
*1938*
*Silver*

HARALD NIELSEN
Ring Nº 46E
*1922*
*Silver*

*Opposite:*
HARALD NIELSEN
Dress Clip Nº 232
*1931*
*Silver*

HARALD NIELSEN
*Garniture de Toilette Nº 4000*
*1942*
*Silver and porcelain*

HARALD NIELSEN
Fish Dish № 600B (cover handle detail)
*1930*
*Silver*

HENNING KOPPEL
Tea Set № 1051
(Teapot, Sugar Bowl, and Creamer)
*1956*
*Silver*

Caravel Teaspoon № 011/33
*1956*
*Silver*

HENNING KOPPEL
Paperweight № 1231,
Pencil Tray № 1232,
Memo-Pad Tray № 1233,
Letter Tray № 1234,
Box № 1236,
Pen Cup № 1243,
Ruler № 394, and
Magnifier № 391
*1978*
*Silver and ebony*

Watch № 392
*1978*
*Stainless steel and black alligator skin*

*Opposite:*
Drawing of the
HENNING KOPPEL
Ruler № 394

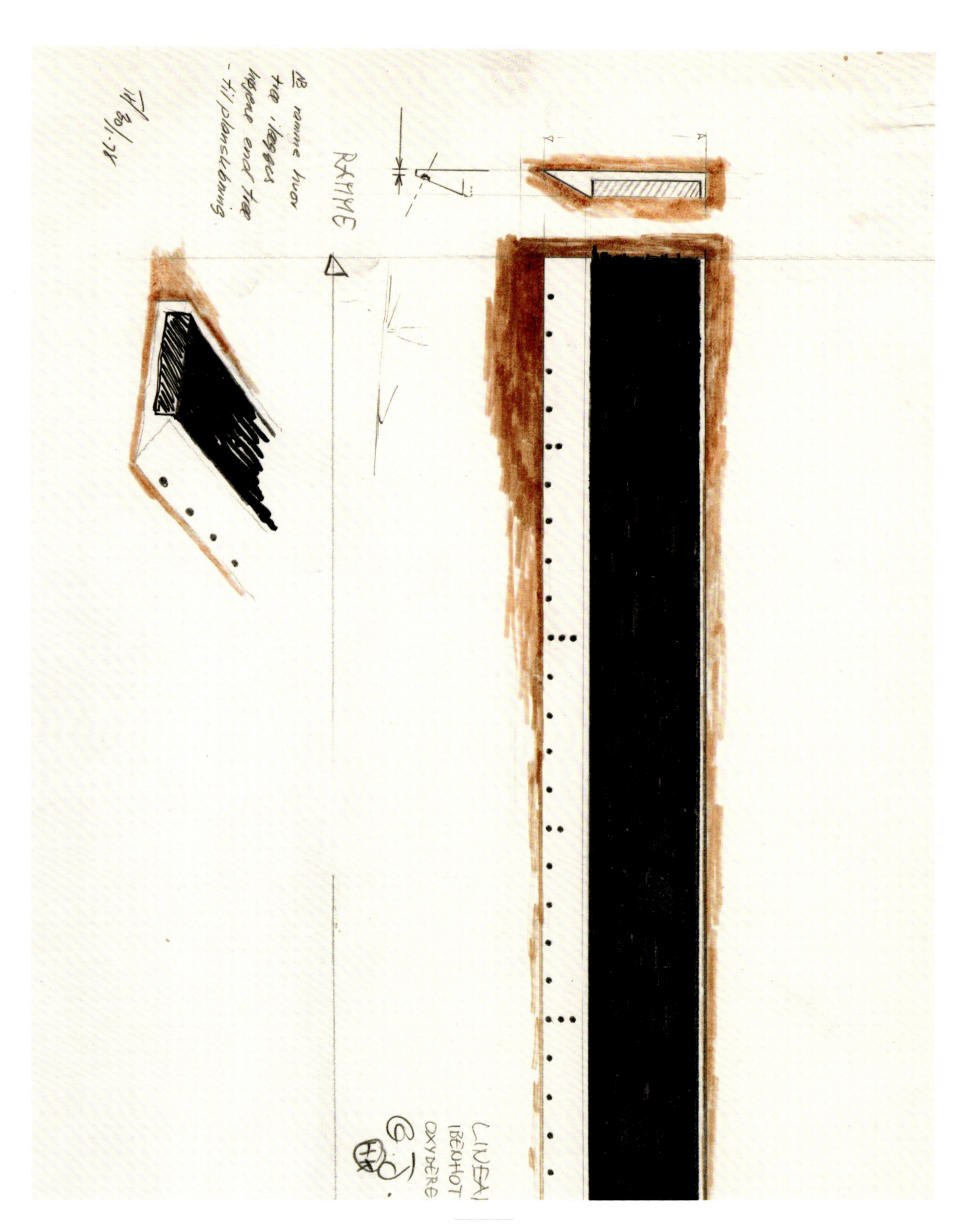

HENNING KOPPEL
Fish Dish № 1026 (detail)
*1954*
*Silver*

# TOUCHING

It is critical, if one wants to truly see a Jensen piece, to touch it—especially the large masterpieces such as the fish platter and jugs of Henning Koppel. One's hands, in this case, have better vision than one's eyes. One must hold them, run one's fingers across the curved surfaces, feel them. The caress is like an X-ray of a Jensen work—it informs what is actually there, and separates the true skeleton of the object from its reflected surface—its skin, which distorts. To explore a Jensen silver masterpiece is like watching a magician show you how a difficult trick, or illusion, is done. The secret may be out, but the magic is in fact not lost, but rather enhanced, because to perform that illusion is in itself seemingly impossible—magic.

Niels-Jørgen Kaiser writes in his book *The World of Henning Koppel*, "He [Koppel] knew down to the last detail what it was he wanted, but he had to see the result and touch it, before he could judge it."

Yet we have been taught not to touch silver, presumably to prevent disturbing the finish of the polished surface. However convenient that argument, it is perverse.

I feel compelled to walk in fresh snow, to rub against velvet, to cut into the cake. Silver is like a mythological Siren—regarding touch, it is a magnet. To touch a Georg Jensen sculpture is like putting your hand into a pond and experiencing the clay bottom—a tactile experience vastly different from the visual experience. If you touch, feel, caress a Jensen piece, you can feel the maker's hands—the weld, the sculpting, the "making." And you instantly understand that each piece of Georg Jensen is unique, because each is made by a unique pair of human hands.

Until you explore, by touch, a piece of Georg Jensen silver, it will remain a secret, a stranger.

HENNING KOPPEL
Fish Dish № 1026
*1954*
*Silver*

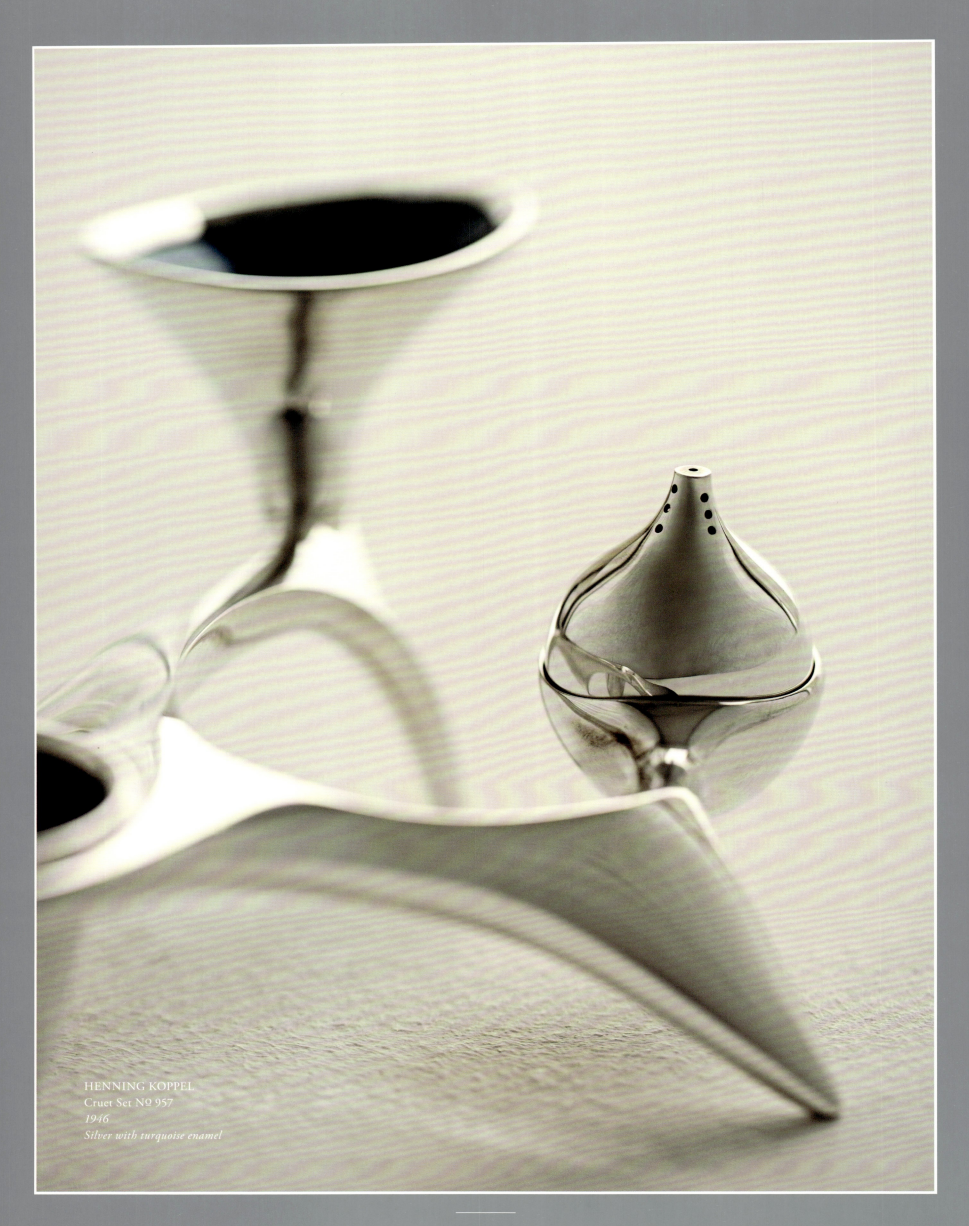

HENNING KOPPEL
Cruet Set № 957
*1946*
*Silver with turquoise enamel*

# THE ESSENCE OF SILVER

Henning Koppel created, on a par with Brancusi and Anish Kapoor, works that arguably rival the most beautiful sculpture of the twentieth century. Working in three dimensions rather than on a flat surface like Munch, Koppel was fascinated by the potency of the reflective curve in metal. Koppel, unlike Jensen who was quoted as saying that silver was obstinate and had to be "conquered," enjoyed—indeed celebrated—the fact that when working in silver, control keeps shifting from maker to material.

Obsessed with creating a new form of silver, and putting aside all pragmatic concerns regarding production, in 1952 Koppel, after long collaboration with the smithery, executed his now-famous Pitcher No. 992.

To me it appears that the pitcher is made of an elastic material, and that when it is filled with water, the jug takes on an extraordinary fluidity, seemingly taking the shape of the liquid inside. The combination of the reflective, distorting silver skin and the bulbous shape that seems to be stretched and filled to capacity—like a warm, sated belly on a cold, cold Nordic night—suggests a container designed more by its contents than by its creator.

Koppel let silver do what it does; rather than conquer it, he mined its properties, pushing the material to perform as it never had before, and let it warp and contort, creating new archetypes for functional objects, giving them new expression through a new visual language. His Fish Dish No. 1026, created in 1954 and over two feet in length, could almost be the model (and most definitely the inspiration) for Indian-British sculptor Anish Kapoor's *Cloud Gate*, the 66-foot-long, elliptical sculpture that is forged of a seamless series of highly polished stainless steel plates which reflect/distort Chicago's famous skyline and the clouds above, as well as the visitors who pass through it.

Both Koppel and Kapoor are inspired by mercury, the only metal that is liquid at standard conditions for temperature and pressure. Koppel and Kapoor defy metal's solid, "obstinate" makeup and demand of it a fluidity that, in both artists' work, results in remarkable tours de force. Challenging the conventional definition of beauty—primarily the worship of symmetry as a necessary ingredient—the asymmetrical reflections in both men's work ironically transform the word "distortion" into its own antonym: clarity, beauty, perfection.

As designer Poul Henningsen explained to his friend Koppel, "It is about being a Romantic struggling against Romanticism."

Vivianna Torun
Bülow-Hübe with
Pablo Picasso, 1955.
The Picasso Museum,
Antibes.

# VIVIANNA TORUN BÜLOW–HÜBE

1927 — 2004

## THE ICONOCLAST

JEWELER / SILVERSMITH / ARTIST

*Friend of Picasso, Matisse, and Braque,*
*Torun (as she was known)*
*was a passionate rule-breaker. She designed*
*hollowware and "anti-status" jewelry*
*of silver, semiprecious stones, and pebbles.*

When she began designing for Georg Jensen in 1967, Vivianna Torun Bülow-Hübe was already on her way to becoming the most celebrated Swedish silversmith of the postwar period. Adding her work to the Jensen oeuvre was like opening a window for the company—fresh air streamed in, along with the wafts of '60s music from Dylan to the Beatles. Her work was deemed "not Jensen" until such time that the company decided it "was Jensen," and then it not only added a new generation but, for me, defined Jensen.

Jensen became hip.

Torun (as she was referred to) was a voice of liberation and equality and multiculturalism of all sorts—women's liberation, social liberation, sexual liberation, racial equality, cultural diversity, and much more.

Growing up on a remote Swedish island, her entire family was creative; it included a sculptor mother, a town planner father, a poet sister, and a brother and other sister who became architects. Torun herself began making jewelry as a teenager. Staging her first exhibition when she was just twenty-one years old, she then traveled to France where she entered the salons of Picasso, Braque, and Matisse. Shortly thereafter, she became the first female silversmith in Sweden to open her own workshop.

Thrice married and divorced—to a Danish journalism student, a French architect, and an African-American painter—she became a member of an international spiritual movement called Subud and in 1968 relocated to Germany to be nearer a Subud community. She later moved to Jakarta, where the movement was founded. At the age of seventy-six Torun passed away in 2004, having moved to Denmark two years before.

Her jewelry was something one wanted to wear (including her smash hit for Jensen—its first watch, *Vivianna*, a bangle-style watch in stainless steel). And she herself was someone one wanted to know.

Beautiful, fearless, willful, sexy, playful, fun, and above all free of most baggage, she was not impressed by money or the trappings it affords, including real gemstones. She was impressed by great art, great artistry, great artists, great freedom.

Jensen, in a sense, got younger; that can happen when a muse enters a room.

Her jewelry? Most revolutionary for Jensen, silver was in many cases made subservient to an ornamental element, usually a crystal or moonstone or pebble which dangled from a post, separating it from the neck ring or bracelet, and giving the piece a composition much like a large exclamation point.

Relegated to being the structure supporting the primitive, tribal-like ornament, the silver elements, rather than quietly receding, were put even more in focus. Ever so thin, subtle, slithery, and sensuous, the silver looked light and fresh, like a blade of grass or a piece of string.

Torun let the sun shine in.

VIVIANNA TORUN
BÜLOW-HÜBE
Neck ring and earrings
VTBH production
*1954*
*Silver and turquoise blue*
*ceramic beads*

VIVIANNA TORUN BÜLOW-HÜBE
Bangle Watch № 326
*1962*
*Stainless steel*

VIVIANNA TORUN BÜLOW-HÜBE
Möbius Brooch № 374
*1968*
*Silver*

VIVIANNA TORUN BÜLOW-HÜBE
Neck Ring № 169, Pendant № 131,
and Bangle № 205
*1968*
*Silver and rock crystal*

VIVIANNA TORUN BÜLOW-HÜBE
Neck Ring with Pendant and Earrings
VTBH production

VIVIANNA TORUN BÜLOW-HÜBE
Neck Ring № 167
*1968*
*Silver*

Pendant № 135
*1968*
*Silver, rock crystal, and amethyst*

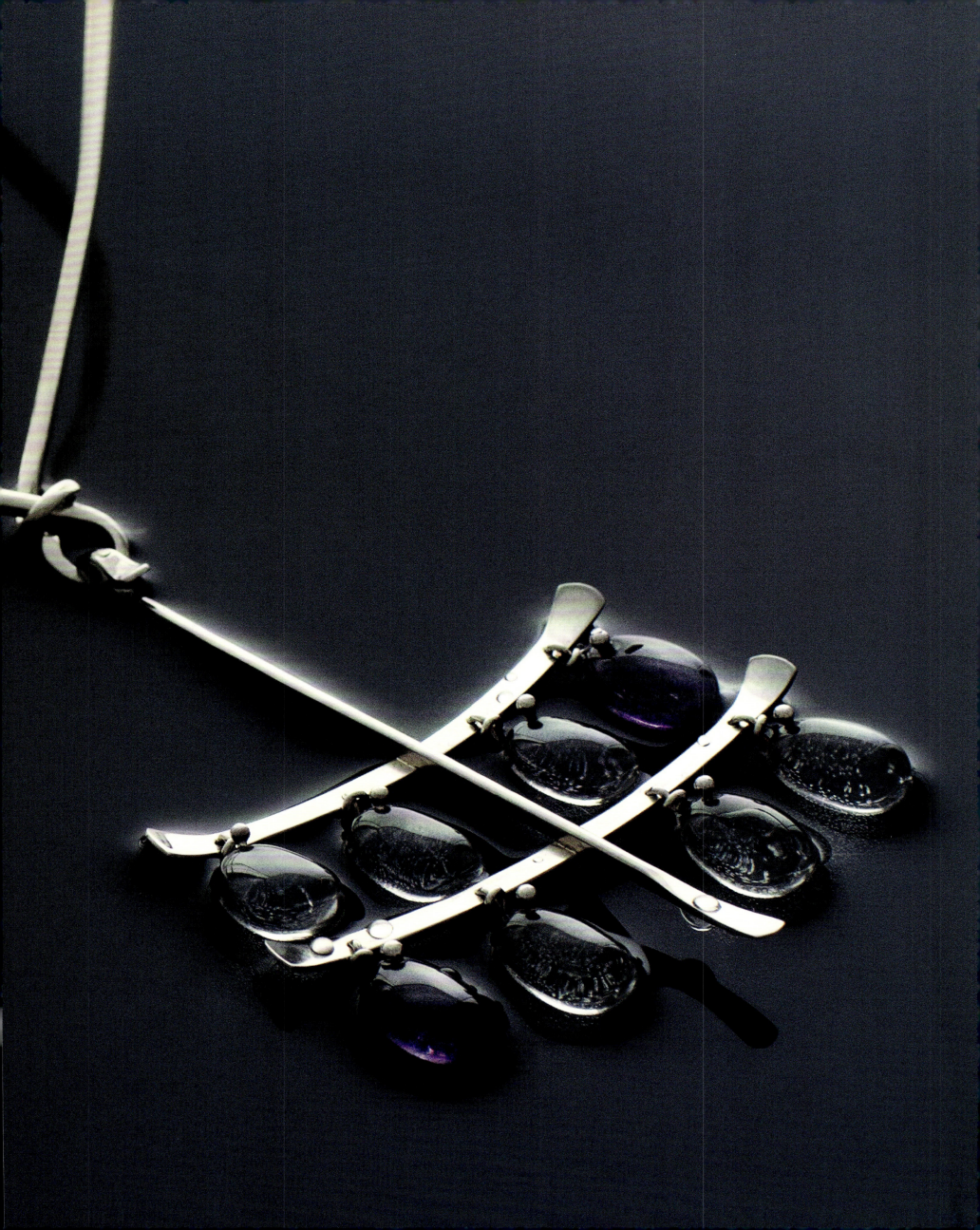

VIVIANNA TORUN BÜLOW-HÜBE
Watch № 229
*1973*
*Silver and quartz*

VIVIANNA TORUN BÜLOW-HÜBE
Ring № 151
*1968*
*Silver and rutilated quartz*

*Opposite:*
VIVIANNA TORUN BÜLOW-HÜBE
Watch № 231
*1974*
*Silver and quartz*

VIVIANNA TORUN BÜLOW-HÜBE
Earrings № 1370
*1998*
*Gold-plated silver*

*Opposite:*
VIVIANNA TORUN BÜLOW-HÜBE
Brooch № 1420
*1971*
*18-karat gold*

VERNER PANTON
Dish Nº 1302 (detail)
*1988*
*Silver*

# VERNER PANTON

1926 – 1998

## THE POP STAR

FURNITURE DESIGNER / LIGHTING DESIGNER /
SILVER DESIGNER

*Panton's designs show an unconventional futuristic flair,
so typical of '60s Pop art. For his* Crash Tray No. 1302, *Panton crushed a piece of paper to show the silversmiths how
he wanted the tray to look: folds, crumples, and all.*

As always, a fully established aesthetic—such as Functionalism in Danish Design in the 1950s—at its apex, triggers a reaction that ushers in yet another aesthetic; design, not exempt from Darwinism, evolves like any other species.

Danish designer Verner Panton's Dish No. 1302, designed in 1988 for Georg Jensen, is a neo-Pop (better late than never!) reexamination of material properties—a pseudo-French reaction against the non-narrative "good taste" palette of Danish Modern. With Dish, an iconoclastic object if ever there was one, Panton commits a kind of luxury-brand hubris by giving a "luxury" material, silver, the form of a piece of trash—neither to denigrate the material nor to offer a cynical comment but rather to neuter the deadening effect of *bon gout* with an eye- (and mind-) opening fresh idea: Silver, in spite of its historical associations that render it "traditional" to say the least, is not in fact under contract to tradition, but, as a free agent, can be used in contemporary design without its bourgeois baggage.

Panton took a sheet of sterling silver and crumpled it like a piece of wastepaper, challenging us to see the potential for art in the banal, much as Duchamp did with the urinal. This was not an arbitrary or amusement-driven act,

but a lesson in looking with an open mind at each object one encounters, without prejudice or bias. Dish, from one perspective, is a brilliant example of the influence of 1980s British-style Heavy Metal/Brutish Butch, as exemplified by British artist/designer Ron Arad's 1983 *Concrete Stereo*. Arad's hi-fi range (record player, speaker, amplifier) is an uncomfortable marriage of technology, which is usually very well dressed, and crumbling concrete and rusted steel—materials normally deemed unworthy of that sector. *Concrete Stereo* and Dish both challenge our sense of physical as well as semiotic propriety in design.

"Look again," Panton instructs. Dish No. 1302 is not a piece of silver trash, but an engineered convex and concave terrain that, like the surface of the moon, generates light through reflection rather than through its own ability to produce light.

With Dish, Panton rocketed silver, and Georg Jensen, through the glass ceiling of tradition and broke the shackles of academia's definition of good taste.

Georg Jensen went to the moon.

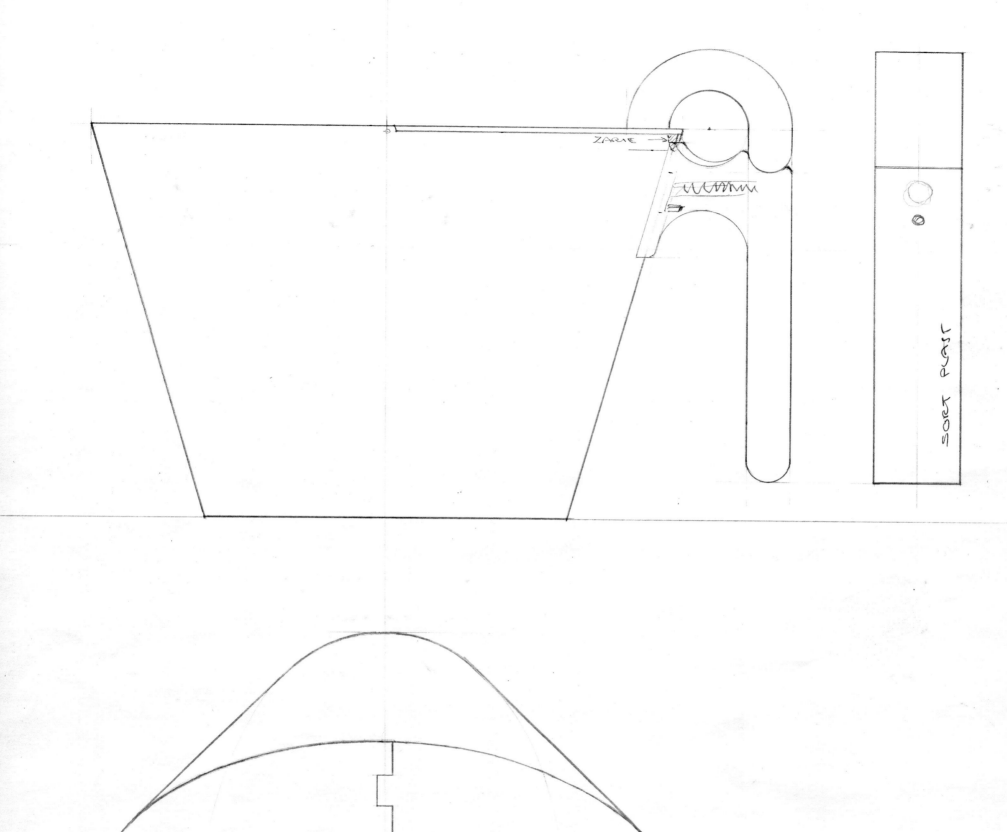

SORT PLAST

ZARIE

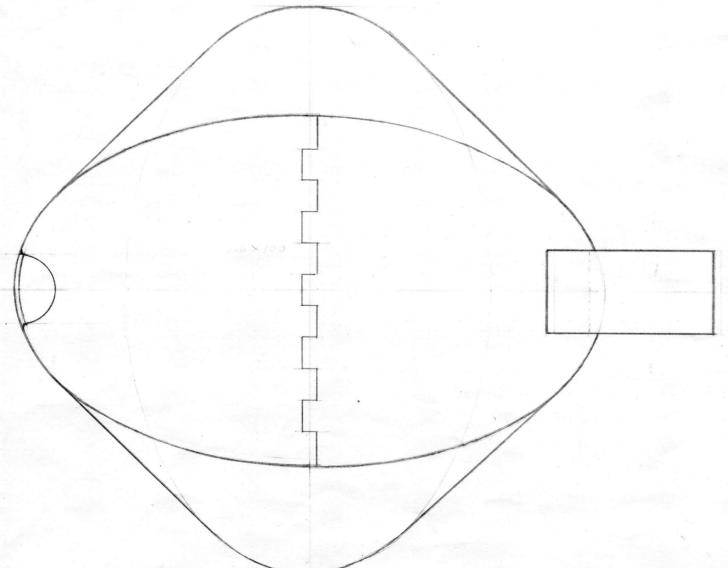

Drawing of the
**VERNER PANTON**
Teapot № 1300

11·1·90

VERNER PANTON
Dish № 1302
*1988*
*Silver*

VERNER PANTON
Coffee and Tea Set № 1300
(Teapot, Coffee Pot, Sugar Bowl, Creamer, and Vase)
*1990*
*Silver and Bakelite*

HENNING KOPPEL
Teapot № 1043
*1954*
*Silver and ivory*

# POLISHING SILVER

I must polish my Jensen sterling silver pieces because sterling silver will tarnish.

Sterling silver is an alloy of silver that consists of 92.5% pure silver and 7.5% other metal, primarily copper. Without the copper, the metal would be too soft for working most models. It is the copper that makes sterling silver much more susceptible to tarnish than pure silver.

Tarnish is a thin layer of corrosion that forms over many metals as the outermost layer undergoes a chemical reaction. Tarnish is a surface phenomenon that is self-limiting (unlike rust); only the top few layers of the metal react, and the layer of tarnish seals and actually protects the underlying layers from reacting.

I polish my Jensen sterling silver so that it maintains its luster. I elect to do this because without my intervention, the chemical reaction, which occurs naturally, will veil the extraordinary and unique beauty of these objects.

Like one's reputation, sterling silver requires vigilance, lest they both tarnish and lose their luster.

There are many things dear in our lives that depend on us for intervention, for maintenance.

John D. Rockefeller, a man who had many things dear in his life, concluded, "I believe that every right implies a responsibility; every opportunity, an obligation; every possession, a duty."

Each of us has a list of those things that we are willing to maintain (things that "imply a duty"), because they bring us joy and because we love them.

Things in life that require pleasurable duties might include: children, physical health, a garden, dogs. And since 1904, many people around the world have added: Georg Jensen silver.

HENNING KOPPEL
Teapot № 1043
*1954*
*Silver and ivory*

# COLLABORATION

## THE ARTISTIC COLLABORATORS
## IN GEORG JENSEN

*Artistic collaboration was a novel concept in 1906. Georg Jensen found stimulation and inspiration in his group of artist friends, often buying sketches from them and turning them into jewelry. Johan Rohde was the first artist to enter into a long-term collaboration with Jensen, beginning in 1906 and lasting until his death in 1935. It set the workshop's standards of mutual respect and shared ideals, which continue to the present day.*

*Below are some of the artists and designers who embraced the collaborative vision:*

GUNDORF ALBERTUS, IB JUST ANDERSEN, SIGVARD BERNADOTTE,

IB BLUITGEN, VIVIANNA TORUN BÜLOW-HÜBE, IBE DAHLQUIST, JØRGEN DITZEL,

NANNA DITZEL, TIAS ECKHOFF, TUK FISCHER, KAY FISKER, ASTRID FOG,

BENT GABRIELSEN, OSCAR GUNDLACH-PEDERSEN, PIET HEIN,

ARNE JACOBSEN, JØRGEN JENSEN, SØREN GEORG JENSEN, EDVARD KINDT-LARSEN,

HENNING KOPPEL, NINA KOPPEL, ARNO MALINOWSKI, ANDREAS MIKKELSEN,

KRISTIAN MØHL-HANSEN, HARALD NIELSEN, REGITZE OVERGAARD,

VERNER PANTON, GUSTAV PEDERSEN, HENRY PILSTRUP, JOHAN ROHDE,

ALLAN SCHARFF, MAGNUS STEPHENSEN

*Where words fail, music speaks.*
—Hans Christian Andersen

In its 110 years of creative output, Georg Jensen has collaborated with an ever-increasing circle of artists, each bringing to the House his or her personality, their personal response to the aesthetic, social, economic, and political factors of their era. This is in fact generally acknowledged to have been key to the Jensen success, having enabled a wide output of magnificent pieces spread across a number of functional categories, priced across a large spectrum, reaching a large number of people, many of whom had previously been excluded from participating in works of such quality.

If I were to attempt to summarize the entire century of Georg Jensen—to try to distill those attributes which compact the depth and breadth of its wide range of stylistic responses to the changing artistic movements of that entire period of time, and to express them in a few key words—it would be daunting.

Hans Christian Andersen writes, "Where words fail, music speaks." So I turn to the language of music.

Given that the word "oeuvre" is a derivation of the Latin "opera," I follow that path and arrive at "aria," a word defined in musical terms as a venue through which characters in the story express feeling. Following this metaphor, Jensen opera has, many times over the past century, constructed and presented us with many arias, some of which are singularly magnificent and distill narrative to a degree that it becomes universal. And within these exceptional arias are certain passages that profoundly challenge the singer's vocal ability, demanding demonstration of extraordinary skill, highly developed craft, imagination, passion, and even physical prowess. These heightened moments in opera are termed "cadenzas" and we listen for them, wait for them, for they set the bar and they define the opera, the oeuvre.

Which are the cadenzas in Jensen?

This book is in fact entirely constructed of what to me are the cadenzas in the 110-year Jensen "opera"—the defining moments. They most definitely include works by Mr. Jensen, Johan Rohde, Harald Nielsen, Sigvard Bernadotte, Henning Koppel, Vivianna Torun Bülow-Hübe, and Verner Panton. These works, culled from the entire Jensen archives and selected for this book, are those particular pieces that inspire me to rise to my feet and shout "Bravo!"

ALLAN SCHARFF
*Ibis* Pitcher № 1328
*1990*
*Silver*

REGITZE OVERGAARD
Bangle Nº 466 (detail)
*2012*
*Silver and black agate*

SØREN GEORG JENSEN
Candelabrum № 1087
*1960*
*Silver*

we have, and the most beautiful. And silver has this lovely moonlight glow. Reminiscent of the light on a Danish summer night. Silver can grow dark, and it can, when it clouds over, resemble the 'bog woman's brew' [the morning mist]."

One of Georg Jensen's trademarks is the unpolished look, which allows the gray-white tone of the silver to come into its own. Where silversmiths once removed all traces of the hammer, Georg Jensen went against the grain, using controlled chasing and strokes of the hammer to add small dimples to the silver, giving the surface a more vivid expression that captures and reflects the light to perfection.

Another thing that has always fascinated me about silver is the laborious and meticulous work process. In a way, it is a relief to me that the silversmiths still sit with their hammers and punches in the smithy in Frederiksberg, making silver objects using the traditional methods. My personal favorites are the *Den Gravide And* (Pregnant Duck) from 1952 and *Fiskefadet* (Fish Dish) from 1954. In these pieces, nothing superfluous interferes with the simple, stringent expression. The latter is universally regarded as a masterpiece, and it takes 450 hours to produce!

On April 19, 2014, Georg Jensen celebrated its 110th anniversary. Today, all silver items are still made with respect for the founder's teachings, and the name has long been synonymous with outstanding design and quality craftsmanship. And though the old traditions of craftsmanship are kept alive, the company is in no way an anachronism, as tradition and renewal go hand in hand. Georg Jensen continues to attract the most talented designers, launch new products, and open stores all over the world. There is so much more to this story than hammered surfaces, clusters of grapes, *Acorn* flatware, and *Daisy* jewelry. Georg Jensen paved the way for a whole new freedom of design. From the beginning, it was clear that Jensen—the man—was extraordinary, someone who would become known as "the man who led Danish silver into a new era." Georg Jensen is an important part of Danish cultural heritage, having long since secured himself a permanent place in international design history.

Remember to look for the silver lining!

*Jesper Bruun Rasmussen*

AUCTION DIRECTOR AND CHAIRMAN, BRUUN RASMUSSEN AUCTIONEERS OF FINE ART

ACKNOWLEDGMENTS

———

I thank Murray Moss, Thomas Loof, Marc Newson, Jesper Bruun Rasmussen, Anne Taylor Davis, Jacob Wildschiødtz, Julie Lysbo Wildschiødtz, Julie Perret, Michael Von Essen, Mariusz Skronski and the Skronski family, Dung Ngo, and Philip Reeser for their contributions to this book, and the team at Georg Jensen with its wide range of expertise: Ida Heiberg Bøttiger, Archive & Event Manager; Kenichi Nakashima, Head of Sales for Georg Jensen Heritage & Silver; Ian David Moore, Head of Georg Jensen Heritage Online; and Robert Wolf, VP Global Public Relations.

Murray Moss joins me in giving particular thanks to Gregory Scott Pepin, Managing Director of Hollowware, Silverware, and Georg Jensen Heritage. Gregory's profound insight and unwavering dedication were paramount in the making of this book.

*David Chu*

CEO, GEORG JENSEN

250